new jewish tunes.

# ruach 5773 songbook

includes CD (also available separately)

TRANSCONTINENTAL
MUSIC Publications
The world's leading publisher of Jewish music since 1938

Visit **www.TranscontinentalMusic.com**
for artist information, educational material, and downloads

RUACH 5773 SONGBOOK: NEW JEWISH TUNES
© 2013 Transcontinental Music Publications
A division of URJ Books and Music
633 Third Avenue, New York, 10017
Tel: 212.650.4105  Fax: 212.650.4119
www.transcontinentalmusic.com – tmp@urj.org
993515

Translations from liturgy from *Mishkan T'fliah* (CCAR Press, 2007). Used with permission. All rights reserved.

Manufactured in the United States of America
Book design and composition by Joel N. Eglash
Typesetting by Josh Wiczer
Cover design by Roy Clark, Pine Point Productions – Windham, ME

ISBN 978-0-8074-1335-7

10 9 8 7 6 5 4 3 2 1

# PREFACE

*RUACH* IS THE HEBREW WORD FOR *SPIRIT*. It is exactly *that* quality which the songs of the *Ruach* series possess. These songs were chosen for their ear-catching melodies, their colorful instrumental support, and for the life the music breathes into their texts. In short, all this is summed up by one common trait: *Ruach*.

The *Ruach* series is the continuation of the seven original NFTY (North American Federation of Temple Youth) albums that were recorded between 1972 and 1989. The NFTY and *Ruach* albums are primary sources of participatory music for cantors, song leaders, musical leaders and all those who disseminate Jewish music. Each *Ruach* CD reflects the spirit, energy, and vibrancy of the Judaism that lives and breathes in the camps, youth groups, and synagogues of the Union for Reform Judaism.

*Joel N. Eglash*
*Series Creator*

Thanks are due to the members of the *Ruach 5773* committee,
whose varying backgrounds and experiences helped shape
this remarkable collection of music, and, of course,
to the artists who have created this great music for all of us.

PROJECT MANAGER
Steve Brodsky

EXECUTIVE COMMITTEE
Cantor Rosalie Will Boxt
Joel N. Eglash

SELECTION COMMITTEE
Aaron Bandler
Adrian Durlester
Rabbi Dan Freelander
Dan Garwood
Emily Kaye Geraci
Michael Goldberg
Adam Karol
Cantor Leigh Korn
Dr. Alan Mason
Jesse Paiken
Mark Pelavin
Dr. Jayson Rodovsky
Cantor Darcie Sharlein
Rachel Wetstein

## HEBREW PRONUNCIATION GUIDE

**VOWELS**

*a* as in *father*

*ai* as in *aisle* (= long *i* as in *ice*)

*e* = short *e* as in *bed*

*ei* as in *eight* (= long *a* as in *ace*)

*i* as in *pizza* (= long *e* as in *be*)

*o* = long *o* as in *go*

*u* = short *u* as in *lunar*

' = unstressed vowel close to ə

or unstressed short *e*

**CONSONANTS**

*ch* as in German *Bach* or
Scottish *loch* (not as in *cheese*)

*g* = hard *g* as in *get* (not soft *g* as in *gem*)

*tz* = as in *boats*

*h* after a vowel is silent

*r* = like the Italian (rolled) or French *r*

# new jewish tunes.

*table of contents*

# ruach 5773

*Page / CD Track

# ruach 5773
## songbook

# all this rain by dan nichols & eighteen

**text & music:** dan nichols

It's Noah.
He's on the boat.
It's the fortieth day.
And he doesn't know it's about to end.

I'm___ just a man,___ the last of my___ kind.

Tenth___ gen-er-a - tion___ born to save time.

I re-mem-ber the sto - ries___ how it was good be-fore

___ Now___ we are flood - ed___

993515

6

993515

# hinei mah tov (eeoohh!)  by  mikey pauker

*how good it is*

**music & english text:** mikey pauker
**hebrew text:** psalm 133:1

> *"Hinei Mah Tov"* is a call for unity. This song, written after a beautiful day of surfing with my friends in Laguna Beach, brings present the absolute blessing of declaring your community and recognizing the fact that all human beings on this earth come from the same source. People from every faith, country, race, and belief system are all brothers and sisters. My translation and the high-energy reggae vibe, produced by the amazing Brian Judah, speak directly to the new generation of Jewish youth and powerfully generate the meaning of the text.

10

993515

*How good and how pleasant it is that*
*brothers / sisters dwell together.*

הִנֵּה מַה־טּוֹב וּמַה־נָּעִים
שֶׁבֶת אַחִים גַּם־יָחַד.

# ayeka *by* chana rothman

*where are you?*

music and english text:
chana rothman
**hebrew text:** chana rothman &
genesis 3:9, 22:1

> Each of us has a story. Each of us is also part of a larger, shared story. Our stories wind through minutes, weeks, summers, lifetimes, and across generations; they unfold through languages ancient and modern. They shape and define us. When we tell and listen to each other's stories with love and respect, we create a deeper understanding of each other and ourselves.
>
> *Ayeka*, a unique word from *Bereshit*/Genesis, asks not just "Where are you?" but a deeper, more soul-searching "Where are you really?" In writing this song, I realized that the answer is *Hineini:* I'm right here. I am living and shaping this story alongside you. My story is with me. Your story is with you. Our story is right here.

**Moderate Funk Rock** (♩ = 120)

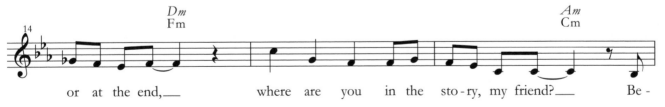

\* Body percussion rhythm:
*Clap / Chest / Chest*
*Clap / Chest / Chest*
*Clap / Chest / Chest / Thighs / Thighs / Stomp / Stomp*

This body percussion pattern is the basis for the whole song and continues throughout the song.

Copyright © 2012 Chana Rothman (ASCAP)

14

993515

Where are you?  I am here.

To life!  To goodness, blessing, and peace.

To life!  To those who work hard every day.

To life!  The end, the middle, or at the beginning:

To life!  Where are we within the main story / plot?

אַיֶּכָּה? הִנֵּנִי.

לְחַיִּים! לְטוֹבָה לִבְרָכָה וּלְשָׁלוֹם.

לְחַיִּים! לְאֵלֶּה שֶׁעוֹבְדִים קָשֶׁה כָּל-יוֹם.

לְחַיִּים! בַּסּוֹף בָּאֶמְצַע אוֹ בַּהַתְחָלָה.

לְחַיִּים! אֵיפֹה אֲנַחְנוּ בְּתוֹךְ הָעֲלִילָה?

# al kein n'kaveh l'cha  by  noam katz

*we therefore hope in you*

**text:** aleinu
**music:** noam katz

"And so we put our hope in You, *Adonai* our God, that we will soon see in the splendor of Your strength, the mending of the world..."

The *Aleinu* (from which these lines are taken) has proved to be one of the more problematic prayers in the history of Jewish worship. Its emphasis on the "chosen" quality of the Jewish people, on that which distinguishes Jews from other nations of the world, has historically been met with suspicion if not aggression. It even causes a stir within our own community, as we so often champion our universalist values and get uncomfortable with what differentiates us as unique and separate. Yet, here in the middle of *Aleinu* appears a simple phrase that weaves together two core pillars of Reform Jewish identity: the belief in one God, which emboldens us to do the work of *tikkun olam*. I felt strongly that this long ignored piece of text should be reintegrated into Reform worship, because it encapsulates who we are and what we prioritize. And so out the melody poured. (I also loved the idea of having God's name hidden inside a *niggun*.)

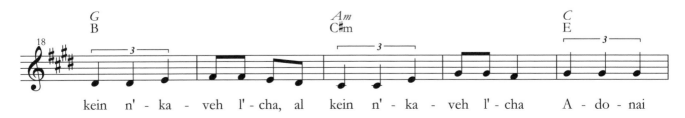

993515

*We therefore hope in You, Adonai our God,*
*may we soon behold the glory of Your might,*
*perfecting the world under the rule of God.*

עַל כֵּן נְקַוֶּה לְךָ יְיָ אֱלֹהֵינוּ,
לִרְאוֹת מְהֵרָה בְּתִפְאֶרֶת עֻזֶּךָ,
לְתַקֵּן עוֹלָם בְּמַלְכוּת שַׁדַּי.

# adonai tzuri v'goali

by **alison westermann**

*adonai, my rock and my redeemer*

**text:** liturgy
**music:** alison westermann

> Sometimes, a song is IN the wind. This song IS the wind. Every breath we take, we breathe these words, "Oh Eternal, my Rock and my Redeemer." This song launched my music career, but it was the one I didn't consciously write! I now believe that this song was given to me as a gift, to remind me at a crucial time in my life of my spiritual connection with the Holy One of Blessing. I invite you to try this song out for yourself, to apply it wherever it feels right in your prayer service (or as a *niggun*!) and to experience the power of this chant. May it transform you as it has transformed me!

*Adonai, my Rock and my Redeemer.*

יְיָ צוּרִי וְגֹאֲלִי.

993515

# halleluyah (live) by josh nelson

*praise god*

**text & music:** josh nelson

Several years back, I suffered a tremendously heartbreaking loss in my life. Needing some time to think and recover, I escaped to a beach in the Dominican Republic. I spent my days getting sunburned, staring at the blank pages of a notebook I'd brought along in hopes of writing about how I was feeling. Days went by, and nothing ended up on those pages except sand and the occasional spilled beverage.

Eventually, I stopped trying to force out the words. I just sat on the beach, closed my eyes, and cried.

When I had no tears left, when my tank was literally empty, I opened my eyes and was greeted by a vista as flawless as I'd ever seen ... a perfect sun, in a perfect sky, over a perfect sea. I was filled with awe, with a sense of real hope… and I knew things would eventually be okay.

I returned home from that trip with the words of this song.

I'm brought back to that beach every time I sing it.

*Baruch Atah, Adonai, Eloheinu Melech haolam, pokeiach ivrim.*

**Laid-back Funk (♩ = 88)**

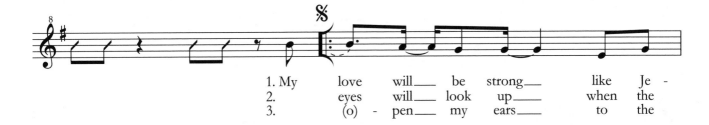

1. My love will__ be strong__ like Je-
2. eyes will__ look up__ when the
3. (o)-pen__ my ears__ to the

ru - sa - lem's sun,__ and my soul,_____ it shines for__ You.
world crash - es down,__ and my soul,_____ it shines for__ You.
sound of__ Your voice,__ and my soul,_____ it shines for__ You.

993515

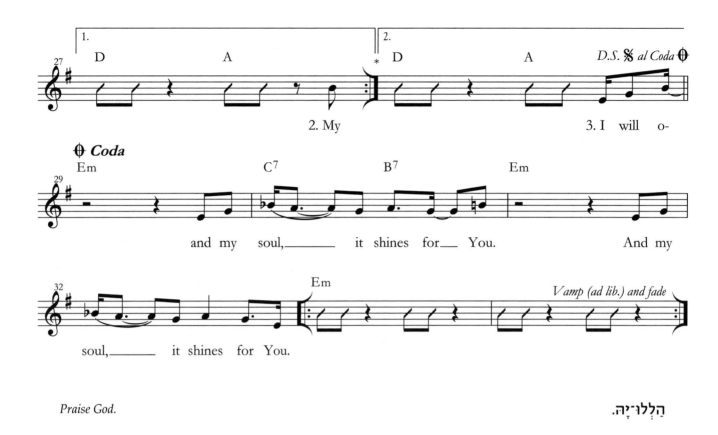

Em
In my heart I be - lieve there are
I will nev - er lose sight of the
I will call out Your name when I'm
C7
chang - es to come, and my soul, it shines for You.
love I have found, and my soul, it shines for You.
mak - ing my choice, and my soul, it shines for You.
Chorus
D B7 C7 B7
Hal - l' - lu, hal - l' - lu,
Em C7 B7
hal - l' - lu - yah. Hal - l' - lu, hal - l' - lu,
Em C7 B7
hal - l' - lu - yah. Hal - l' - lu, hal - l' - lu,
Em 3 C7 B7 To Coda
hal - l' - lu - yah, and my soul, it shines for You.
Em

*Praise God.*

הַלְלוּ־יָהּ.

---

\* As per the recording, an optional instrumental break may be inserted here.

# thank you     by   naomi less

*modah ani*

**english text & music:** naomi less
**hebrew text:** morning liturgy

> One day, I came home experiencing a great buzz that life was moving in a direction I was digging. I sat down on the couch and wrote a list of the things I was grateful for—some obvious, like my nephews calling me from St. Paul on their way to school, and some not so obvious, like lessons I still need to learn or a delay on the subway. It hit me: this is *Modah Ani*—when you wake up first thing in the morning and set your intentions towards gratitude. It's amazing how different your day can be when you start off from a place of thanks rather than a place of need. What's on your list? Give it a try.

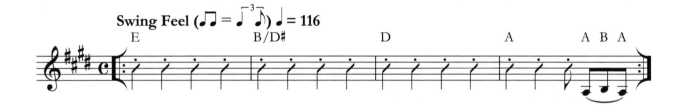

1. For the way that I breathe   For the loves in my life

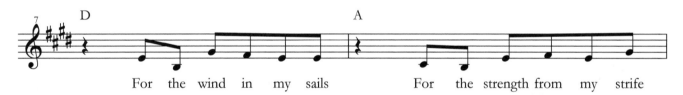

For the wind in my sails   For the strength from my strife

For the les - sons I still___ need___ the ones I have

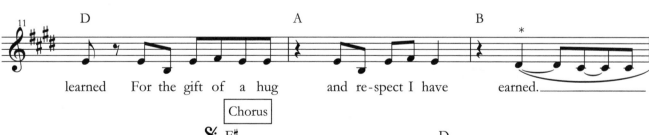

learned   For the gift of a hug   and re-spect I have   earned.___

Chorus

Mo - dah a - ni l' - fa - ne - cha,___

\* = As in the accompanying recording, syllables are sometimes repeated or "re-vocalized" on succeeding notes. The word appears only on the first note in these instances.

993515

24

*I offer thanks to You,*
*that You have restored my soul in me.*

מוֹדָה אֲנִי לְפָנֶיךָ,
שֶׁהֶחֱזַרְתָּ בִּי נִשְׁמָתִי

# beauty of the world by sababa

*shekacha lo b'olamo*

**hebrew text:** traditional blessing
for rare beauty
**english text and music:** steve brodsky,
scott leader, robbi sherwin

ruach
57 73
track 8

While writing the songs for our second CD, *It's All Good*, we were camped out in the beautiful Denver home of some close friends. The house sits on a hill and has huge windows that frame the Rocky Mountains to the west. As the sun sank that evening, the sky was ablaze with the incredible oranges, blues, purples, and pinks of a stunning Colorado sunset. This awesome display brought to mind the prayer one says when seeing something of rare beauty: *Baruch Atah Adonai, Eloheinu Melech ha'olam, shekacha lo b'olamo*: "Blessed are you, God, who puts such things in the world." This simple yet powerful blessing reminds us to always be aware of and grateful for the beautiful world that God has created.

Copyright © 2010 Sababa

27

* = Per the recording, the final chorus may be repeated.

993515

28

*Blessed are You, Adonai our God, Sovereign of the Universe,*
*Who puts such things in the world.*

בָּרוּךְ אַתָּה יְיָ אֱלֹהֵינוּ מֶלֶךְ הָעוֹלָם,
שֶׁכָּכָה לוֹ בְּעוֹלָמוֹ.

# ana el na by jaffa road

*please, heal her*

**text:** based on numbers 12:13
**music:** aaron lightstone,
aviva chernick, chris gartner,
michael rennie

> Composed by the members of Jaffa Road with some input from Mike Rennie, a South African musician living in California, "Ana El Na" is a hypnotic six-word chant recalling Moses' plaintive cry to God for the healing of his sister Miriam when she is stricken with leprosy. These words, from Numbers 12:13, translate as "Please heal her!" This recording features the voices of Aviva Chernick and Mike Rennie, with layers of vocal harmony, accompanied by oud, bass, bansuri, synthesisers, drums and percussion. "Ana El Na" was recently honored by Folk Music Ontario with an award in their annual Songs from the Heart Songwriting Contest.

993515

30

\* Melody in bars 1-2 can be repeated here (under the voice).

993515

*Please, God, heal her now.*

אָנָּא אֵל נָא רְפָא נָא לָהּ.

# mi chamocha   by  hannah spiro

*who is like you*

**english text & music:** hannah spiro
**hebrew text:** morning liturgy

> I grew up with a Reform *siddur* that treated *Mi Chamochah* as a pure and simple celebration of freedom. I remember my shock when I first realized that the traditional liturgy of *Mi Chamochah* is about hundreds of horsemen and horses drowning in the sea as the Israelites celebrate their relief: they're not going to be put back in slavery; everything is going to be okay. It's an intense image — very bitter, and yet very sweet. In setting out to write my own interpretation of *Mi Chamochah*, I tried to capture both of those feelings, and played with navigating a way for us to both celebrate and reflect.

Copyright © 2012 Hannah Spiro

* = As in the accompanying recording, syllables are sometimes repeated or "re-vocalized" on succeeding notes. The word appears only on the first note in these instances.

ay - yai - yai,____ who can do____ (oo - oo - oo) the things you do?

Oo - ah, Mi cha-mo-chah ba - ei-lim, A - do-nai! Oo - ah, Mi ka-mo-chah

ne - dar ba-ko - desh.

Who is like You, O God, among the gods that are worshipped?

Who is like You, majestic in holiness,

awesome in splendor, working wonders!

A free people

With new song, inspired at the shore of the Sea,

the redeemed sang Your praise.

In unison they all offered thanks.

Acknowledging Your Sovereignty, they said:

"Adonai will reign forever!"

מִי כָמְכָה בָּאֵלִם, יְיָ!

מִי כָּמְכָה נֶאְדָּר בַּקֹּדֶשׁ,

נוֹרָא תְהִלֹּת, עֹשֵׂה פֶלֶא!

בְּנֵי חוֹרִין

שִׁירָה חֲדָשָׁה

שִׁבְּחוּ גְאוּלִים

לְשִׁמְךָ עַל שְׂפַת הַיָּם.

יַחַד כֻּלָּם הוֹדוּ וְהִמְלִיכוּ וְאָמְרוּ:

יְיָ יִמְלֹךְ לְעוֹלָם וָעֶד.

# echad  by noah aronson

*one*

text & music: noah aronson

After having written "Am I Awake" and performing it in numerous communities, I was struck by how many people were affected by the personal nature of those words. So I set out to write a musical response to that piece.

If "Am I Awake" is a *midrash* on the *Bar'chu*, then "Echad" is meant to be a personal reflection on the *Sh'ma* and *V'ahavta*. Where "Am I Awake" asks a question, "Echad" delivers its message in the imperative: "Wake up!" for there is nothing more central to our faith then the concept of *Echad* — of unity, of oneness. It is only when we've affirmed our commitment to *Echad* that we can begin to comprehend the weighty commandment of *V'ahavta*.

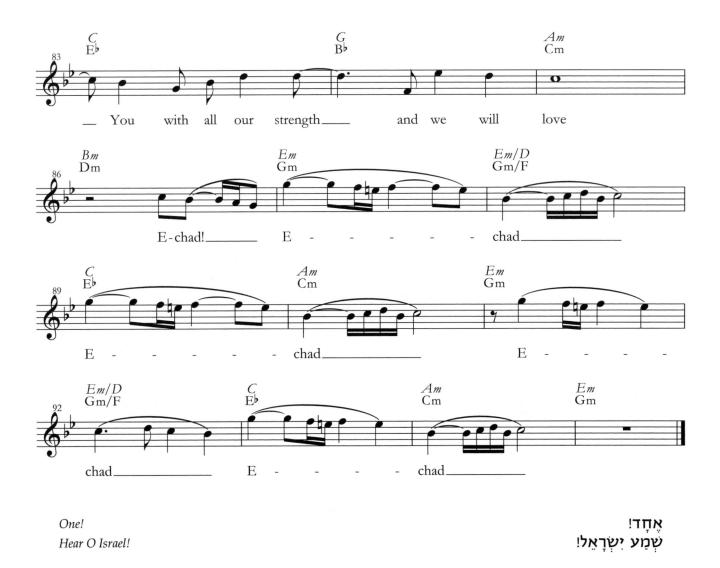

One!
Hear O Israel!

אֶחָד!
שְׁמַע יִשְׂרָאֵל!

# mayim by **dan nichols and eighteen**

*water*

**text:** isaiah 12:3
**music:** dan nichols

> This song was written and developed on the Road to Eden Deep South *Sukkot* Tour, a 2,600-mile road trip and concert tour through the Deep South that my band and I began in October 2011. The tour was designed to shine a light on the deeper meaning of the holiday of *Sukkot*, which expresses many of the Jewish tradition's most profound teachings about our connection to the earth, the fragility of existence, and the hope for redemption. *Sukkot* is about taking action and committing ourselves to realizing our dream of a world perfected. Sukkot says: we are all in this together, walking the Road to Eden.
>
> The text, from Isaiah 12:3, is traditionally used during *Sukkot*: "Joyfully shall you draw water from the wells of your salvation."
>
> *Road to Eden: Rock & Roll Sukkot*, a feature film chronicling the tour, is scheduled for a *Sukkot* 2013 release (more info at roadtoedentour.com).

993515

# l'chu n'ranena *by* soulaviv

*come, let us sing joyously*

**text:** psalm 95:1-2
**music:** robert raede

> This is Psalm 98, and *L'chu N'ranena* essentially means "go and rejoice." We tried to capture that joyous celebration in this setting, using rhythms from the Jewish Diaspora in Jamaica.

**Jamaican "Dance Hall" Groove (♩ = 93)**

oo, _____ oo, _____ oo, _____ oo, _____

_____ oo, _____ oo, _____ oo, _____ oo.

L'-chu n'- ra - n'- nah la - do - nai na - ri - ah l'- tzur yi -

shei - nu, l'- tzur yi - shei - nu. L'-chu n'- ra - n'- nah la - do -

nai na - ri - ah l'- tzur yi - shei - nu, l'- tzur yi - shei - nu. L'-chu n'-

ra - n'- nah la - do - nai na - ri - ah l'- tzur yi - shei - nu, l'- tzur yi -

shei - nu. L'-chu n'- ra - n'- nah la - do - nai, na - ri - ah l'- tzur yi -

47

993515

shei - nu,  l' - tzur  yi - shei - nu.  oo,_____ oo,_____

oo,_____  oo,_____  oo,_____

oo,_____  oo,_____  oo.

Come, let us sing joyously to Adonai,
raise a shout for our Rock and Deliverer;
let us come into God's presence with praise;
let us raise a shout for God in song!

לְכוּ נְרַנְּנָה לַיְיָ,
נָרִיעָה לְצוּר יִשְׁעֵנוּ.
נְקַדְּמָה פָנָיו בְּתוֹדָה,
בִּזְמִרוֹת נָרִיעַ לוֹ.

# ein kamocha  by  eric komar

*there is none like you*

text: psalms 86, 93, 29; exodus 15
music: eric komar

Rejoice in the Torah! This setting of *Ein Kamocha* was composed in 2010 for the son of a rabbi with whom I have the privilege of working, on the occasion of his Bar Mitzvah. My choice of text was motivated by an interest in "spicing up" the Torah service, which, in my opinion, has unnecessarily fallen behind other parts of the worship service in terms of abundance of lively contemporary repertoire. (Listeners are encouraged to check out my "L'cha Adonai," which was composed for the same purpose). Based on my own experience implementing this song, it not only works in the lead-up to removing the Torah from the Ark, but also makes for a lively *hakafah*. Your congregations will love it!

**Middle-Eastern feel** ♩ = 112

1. Ein___ ka-mo-cha___ va - E - lo - him,___ A - do - nai,___ v'-ein k'-ma-a-

se - cha._____ Ma - l' - chut - cha___ mal-chut kol_____

o - la - mim___ u - mem - shalt - cha___ b' - chol dor___ va - dor.___

Chorus

A - do - nai me - lech,___ A - do - nai ma - lach,___ A - do -

nai yim - loch l' - o - lam va - ed.___ A - do -

\* = E Ahavah Rabbah mode

993515

There is none like You among the gods, Adonai,
and there are no deeds like Yours.
You are Sovereign over all worlds,
and Your dominion is in all generations.
Adonai reigns, Adonai has reigned,
Adonai will reign forever and ever.
Adonai will give strength to our people,
Adonai will bless our people with peace.

אֵין כָּמוֹךָ בָאֱלֹהִים אֲדֹנָי,
וְאֵין כְּמַעֲשֶׂיךָ.
מַלְכוּתְךָ מַלְכוּת כָּל־עֹלָמִים,
וּמֶמְשַׁלְתְּךָ בְּכָל־דֹּר וָדֹר.
יְיָ מֶלֶךְ, יְיָ מָלָךְ,
יְיָ יִמְלֹךְ לְעֹלָם וָעֶד.
יְיָ עֹז לְעַמּוֹ יִתֵּן,
יְיָ יְבָרֵךְ אֶת עַמּוֹ בַשָּׁלוֹם.

# boi kalah  by  aviva chernick

*come in, bride*

**text:** chaim nachman bialik
**music:** aviva chernick
and chris gartner

> Growing up, we sang a lovely melody to this exquisite poem welcoming Shabbat, but a dear friend suggested that a new version of this tune was in order. During a trip to Namibia in 2011, this melody came to me. There, in the 40 degree weather, with the syllables "hey" and "ho," I had no idea that this was to be my new framing for Chaim Nachman Bialik's poem that so beautifully welcomes the Sabbath Bride. This melody now fills our home as we gather on Friday nights around the Shabbat table and I have the pleasure of hearing audiences around the world sing it in full voice. I hope you enjoy!

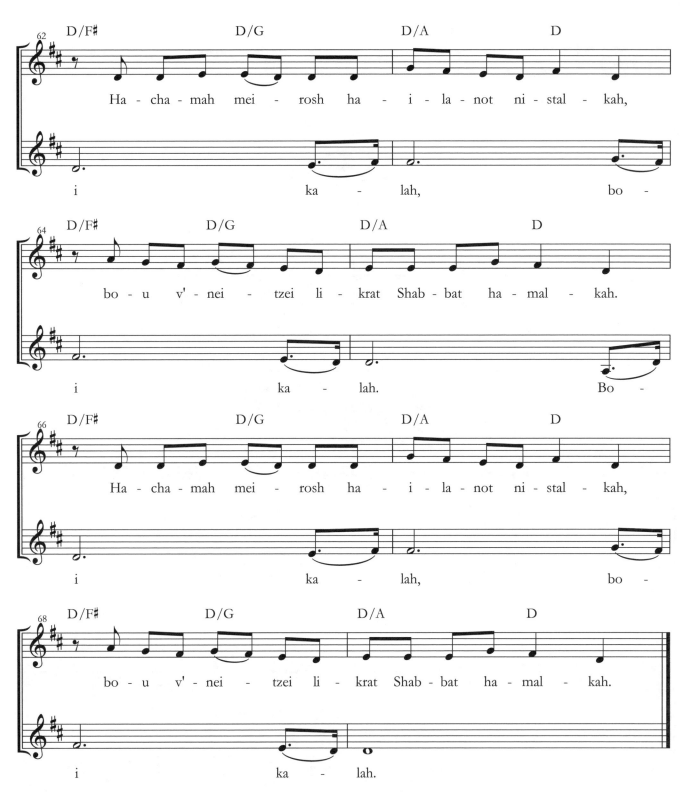

*Come in, bride. Come in, bride.*
*The sun from above the treetops has faded,*
*won't you come with me to greet the Sabbath Queen.*
*Here she descends, the holy one, the blessed one,*
*and with her an army of peaceful messengers.*

בּוֹאִי כַלָּה, בּוֹאִי כַלָּה.
הַחַמָּה מֵרֹאשׁ הָאִילָנוֹת נִסְתַּלְקָה
בּוֹאוּ וְנֵצֵא לִקְרֵאת שַׁבָּת הַמַּלְכָּה.
הִנֵּה הִיא יוֹרֶדֶת הַקְּדוֹשָׁה הַבְּרוּכָה
וְעִמָּהּ מַלְאָכִים צְבָא שָׁלוֹם וּמְנוּחָה.

# halleluyah  by  rick recht

text & music: rick recht

We are all so fortunate to be teachers and learners — each and every one of us. As human beings, this is truly one of our greatest gifts. We all have the amazing opportunity to connect with each other, whether in an academic environment, on a *bima*, on a stage, or in a conversation with a loved one. Children, teens, and adults are all blessed with this unique ability and when we recognize how unbelievably fortunate we are to share and impact each other in these ways, we speak this word that says it all: Halleluyah!

993515

*Praise God, I will praise.*

הַלְלוּ־יָה, הַלְלִי.

# artist biographies

**NOAH ARONSON** is an energetic and soulful composer and performer whose unique musical style has propelled his music into communities across America and in Israel. While studying piano and jazz composition at Berklee College of Music in Boston, Noah served as composer-in-residence at Temple Beth Elohim in Wellesley, Massachusetts, where he taught and composed a wide array of new liturgical works. Noah conducted the Manhattan HaZamir Choir from 2008 to 2010 and his choral music received an honorable mention in the 2009 Guild of Temple Musicians Young Composer's Contest. Noah released his first solo album of contemporary Jewish music, *Am I Awake*, in 2011 and the title song was the winner of the 2011 NewCAJE NewVoices song competition. He is a founding member of the Jewish artists' collective NuRootz as well as a member of the award-winning *a cappella* group Six13. In 2012, Noah became rabbinic intern/chazzan sheni at Temple Beth Elohim and will soon begin the journey towards becoming a rabbi. www.noaharonson.com.

♦ ♦ ♦ ♦ ♦ ♦

**AVIVA CHERNICK**'s intoxicatingly soulful vocals are a wondrous celebration of the beauty of the human voice. Whether on tour with Juno Award-nominated world music ensemble Jaffa Road, as a cantorial soloist leading prayer in synagogues from Toronto to Los Angeles, or on her newly released debut solo recording of original Jewish music for prayer *when i arrived you were already there*, Aviva's engagement with congregations around North America has been an inspiration for her musical adventures. Aviva sings, writes, records, and performs a combination of world music in Hebrew, Ladino, English, Arabic, and French. Shaped by years of sharing devotional songs of peace and prayer with worldwide audiences, her growing body of work reveals a tireless force of nature. www.avivachernick.com.

♦ ♦ ♦ ♦ ♦ ♦

Based in Toronto, **JAFFA ROAD** is an award-winning world music group made up of some of Canada's most exciting and innovative interpreters of inter-cultural music. The group creates a unique sonic landscape that draws easily and organically from the worlds of Jewish music, Arabic and Indian music, modern jazz, electronica, rock, pop, and dub—creating a powerful union between acoustic and electronic, secular and sacred, ancient and modern. The band's second CD *Where the Light Gets In* was recently released to critical acclaim. Their song "L.Y.G." from their debut album *Sunplace* won Grand Prize and a Lennon Award in the prestigious John Lennon Songwriting Contest and the band was awarded Best World Music Artist at the 2010 Toronto Independent Music Awards. They have traveled to many communities across Canada delighting audiences with their unique brand of genre-bending fusion. www.jaffaroad.com.

# artist biographies

Rabbi **NOAM KATZ**, MAJE, is a lifelong educator, prayer leader, and songleader. He has performed at camps and congregations across North America, Israel, and Africa, bringing his passion for Jewish text, social justice, and world music. Noam has released three albums of original Jewish tunes: *Rakia; Mirembe, Salaam v'Shalom*; and his latest release, *A Drum In Hand*. He currently serves in a pioneering role as the Dean of Jewish Living for URJ Camp George and The Leo Baeck Day School in Toronto. He forms one-half of the duo Tof B'yad with his friend Mike Mason, bringing the energy of drum circles and global rhythms into the Jewish prayer experience. And he enjoys most kinds of ice cream. www.noamkatz.com.

◆ ◆ ◆ ◆ ◆ ◆

Listeners of all ages have enjoyed the folk- and jazz-tinged Jewish rock of **ERIC KOMAR**. The veteran singer-songwriter-guitarist performs at synagogues, JCCs, and Hillels nationwide, and has appeared at CAJE and URJ Biennial conventions. Eric's debut CD *Notes from the Underground* (2003) contains the peace anthem "Lo Yisa Goi" as well as "Don't Give Up the Hope," a solo guitar rendition of the Israeli National Anthem. His second effort *Two Life* (2007) features the social action anthem "Justice, Justice." He ushered in 2011 with his third CD *Ripples*, from which "Ein Kamocha," his song appearing in this Ruach compilation, was drawn. Eric lives in New Jersey with his wife, two kids, and two cats. In addition to performing and recording Jewish music, he serves as the music specialist at a number of local synagogues, works in the field of music publishing, and teaches guitar. www.komarmusic.com.

◆ ◆ ◆ ◆ ◆ ◆

**NAOMI LESS** is a songwriter, activist, educator, and top touring Jewish female rock musician who inspires and empowers audiences across the generations worldwide to own their Jewish identities. She melds pop-rock riffs and soulful anthems with lyrics that explore self-worth, theology, and the Jewish experience. Naomi uses music as a platform to speak out on bullying and gender equality, igniting and engaging social activism. "Jewish Chicks Rock" and "Jewish Kids Rock" are Naomi's signature educational rock music programs for camps, JCC's and schools, are designed to empower the next generation to create justice and values-based music. Naomi has certificates and degrees in Jewish education and facilitation from JTS, Brandeis University, Institute for Jewish Spirituality, and Center for Leadership Initiatives, and serves as musician-in-residence at three New York synagogues. She is also a founding company member and maven trainer for Storahtelling. www.naomiless.com.

◆ ◆ ◆ ◆ ◆ ◆

**JOSH NELSON** is one of the most popular performers and producers in modern Jewish music. A multi-instrumentalist and songwriter, Josh's music is celebrated and integrated into the repertoire

# artist biographies

of congregations, camps, and communities around the world. Josh's work combines a message of Jewish identity and continuity with extraordinary musicality, razor-sharp lyricism, and a progressive, radio-ready sound. Josh has performed over one thousand shows in a variety of venues, including international conventions for each of the major youth movements in the USA (NFTY, USY, BBYO, etc.), URJ Biennial Conventions, Limmud Conferences, JCCA National Conventions, JCC Maccabi Games, CAJE Conferences, and JCCs across the country. Josh serves as the music director for the URJ Biennial Convention, faculty for the Hava Nashira Music Institute, and a musical artist in residence for the JCC Maccabi Artsfest. www.joshnelsonproject.com.

◆ ◆ ◆ ◆ ◆ ◆

**DAN NICHOLS** is a singular talent in the world of Jewish music. He is one of the most dynamic, influential, and beloved Jewish musicians in North America. Dan's melodies have become an integral part of the spiritual and liturgical experience of countless individuals and Jewish communities. Dan's anthology includes a wide range of sounds and styles, from energetic Jewish rock anthems to moving interpretations of traditional Jewish liturgy. Jewish youth and adults from around the world draw inspiration from Dan's music and its positive message of Jewish values, identity, and pride. Dan spends more than 180 days each year on the road, often serving as artist-in-residence for congregations and camp communities. In 2011 Dan created the "Road to Eden Deep South Sukkot Tour" to bring the music and message of Sukkot to numerous communities in the southern United States, where he and his band played 11 shows in 10 days. Their experiences will be captured in the forthcoming film, *Road to Eden: Rock & Roll Sukkot*. Dan lives in Raleigh, North Carolina, with his wife Elysha and his daughter Ava. www.jewishrock.com.

◆ ◆ ◆ ◆ ◆ ◆

**MIKEY PAUKER** has been described as one of the most profound and trend-setting Jewish recording artists and experiential educators in the world. Recognized as an engaging musician who is transforming the boundaries of contemporary Jewish music and generating "Jewish cross-over music," Mikey draws inspiration from traditional Jewish liturgy, *Chassidut*, mysticism, and his own Jewish experiences. Mikey serves as an artist-in-residence for BBYO's CLTC summer program in West Virginia, and travels all over the country throughout the year songleading and teaching Jewish yoga and meditation. Recently he has shared the stage with Matisyahu, Moshav, Trevor Hall, Idan Raichel, Yael Mayer, Josh Nelson, and Craig Taubman, among others. Mikey's "Sim Shalom" was featured in the *Ruach 5771* collection and has been implemented in congregations, youth groups, and summer camps all over the U.S. and Israel. Currently Mikey is hard at work on a full-length record with producer Diwon (Y-Love, Bonhom; owner of PR Agency and recording label Shemspeed), with an expected release in 2013. www.mikeypauker.com.

# artist biographies

**RICK RECHT** is one of the top touring musicians in Jewish music, playing over 150 concerts a year in the United States and abroad. Recht is widely recognized for his appeal to youth and family audiences not only as an exceptional musician, singer/songwriter, and entertainer, but also as a role model for involvement in Jewish life. He has become an icon for Jewish youth in the United States, elevating the medium of Jewish music as a powerful and effective tool for developing Jewish pride and identity among the masses. Recht is the national music spokesman for The PJ Library and the executive director of Songleader Boot Camp, a national leadership development immersion program held annually in St. Louis, Missouri. Recht is also the founder and executive director of Jewish Rock Radio, the first high-caliber Jewish rock internet radio station, streaming 24/7 at www.jewishrockradio.com. www.rickrecht.com.

◆ ◆ ◆ ◆ ◆ ◆

Music and vibrant Jewish life have brought singer/songwriter, songleader, and educator **CHANA ROTHMAN** around the world, from Philadelphia's "World Cafe Live" to global workshops and concerts throughout Europe, Israel, and South Africa. Chana's music is a unique blend of folk, world-beat, and hip-hop, aiming to break down barriers and move the world towards consciousness and change. Chana has released two albums of original Jewish music, *We Can Rise* (2007) and *Beautiful Land* (2011), both produced by Grammy award-winner C Lanzbom (Pete Seeger, Soulfarm). Chana is also commissioned annually by the Foundation for Jewish Camp's Cornerstone Fellowship to write a song that reflects positive role modeling; these songs are bilingual/bicultural and speak to the hunger for meaningful lyrics as young Jews build their sense of identity. "Ayeka" was one of these songs. Recently, Chana joined "Real Women * Real Songs," a community of female songwriters who have each committed to write a song each week for 52 weeks (facebook.com/realwomenrealsongs). Chana performed at Colorado's Telluride Bluegrass Festival in 2012 as a finalist in the Troubadour competition. Chana believes in and lives by building community through music. www.chanarothman.com.

◆ ◆ ◆ ◆ ◆ ◆

**SABABA** is an Arabic word that has become widely used as Israeli slang, meaning "really cool" or "awesome." Sababa is also Steve Brodsky, Scott Leader, and Robbi Sherwin, three accomplished songwriters, performers, and recording artists who joined forces in 2006 to create great, rockin' new Jewish music. They are from three different cities and three different time zones (Denver, Phoenix, and Austin), but that can't stop their energetic spirited Jewish songcrafting from making its way to camps, synagogues, Jewish festivals, churches, and JCCs around the world. Sababa recently released *Shalosh*, their third album in five years. They are known for their masterful musicianship, state-of the art production, and for their impeccable Crosby, Stills, and Nash-like harmonies. www.sababamusic.com.

# artist biographies

**SOULAVIV** was formed in 2007, and in a few short years has earned a reputation as "One of the most exciting new vocal groups in Jewish music" (LA *Examiner*, 9/16/2011). Equally at ease singing in English, Hebrew, and even Yiddish, SoulAviv's music is infused with the sounds of Motown, gospel, Memphis soul, and a particular love for the great harmony groups of the 60's and 70's. Socially conscious lyrics mixed with deep spirituality, jubilant celebration, and a little California sunshine make SoulAviv a unique musical experience that is contemporary yet timeless. www.soulaviv.com.

◆ ◆ ◆ ◆ ◆ ◆

Folk-pop melodies meet textual tradition in **HANNAH SPIRO**'s alt-Jewish tunes. With her recordings *It Is Upon Us* (2012) and *Aliyah* (2010), Hannah combines progressive *midrash* and interpretive liturgy with the musical sentiment of a 90's kid raised on Fleetwood Mac and bubblegum pop. Hannah has been featured as an Emerging Artist on Jewish Rock Radio and has shared the stage with artists ranging from Pete Seeger to Flory Jagoda to Rick Recht. Hannah is thrilled to visit congregations for musical Shabbat services and artist residencies, and loves raising consciousness and energy levels among adults, teens, and kids alike. Hannah recently began rabbinic studies at the Reconstructionist Rabbinical College in Philadelphia, PA. www.hannahspiro.com.

◆ ◆ ◆ ◆ ◆ ◆

**ALISON WESTERMANN**'s music may come from a dark place (the sudden death of her sister), but it brings light into the world. After experiencing this terrible loss, Alison tried to push away the outside world but the music kept whispering in her ear, demanding to be sung and shared. The result is her debut album *Shapirit/Dragonfly*, titled in honor of her sister Lauren's favorite insect. Alison sings at home with her family and congregation in El Paso, Texas, as well as around the U.S. as a guest artist-in-residence in congregations and community centers. www.alisonwestermann.com.

# Catch some Ruach!

*Ruach 5773* is the latest in the classic series of Songbook + CD sets from Transcontinental Music Publications. Released every two years since 2001, the *Ruach* series features the newest, coolest Jewish rock music from established and emerging Jewish artists, some that are already your favorites, and others that you will come to love. Check out the entire series at www.transcontinentalmusic.com/ruachseries

**Ruach 5771**
Featuring 19 tunes from:
- Elana Jagoda
- Dan Nichols & Eighteen
- Michelle Citrin
- Soul Aviv
- Steve Meltzer
- The Levins
- Jay Rapoport
- Peri Smilow
- Mikey Pauker
- Jeremy Gimbel & Shira Tirdof
- Cantor Natalie Young
- Ross M. Levy
- Josh Nelson
- Alan Goodis
- Jon Nelson & Yom Hadash
- Craig Taubman
- Rick Recht
- Max Chaiken & Camp Harlem

**Ruach 5769**
Featuring 18 tunes from:
- Michelle Citrin
- Dan Nichols & Eighteen
- Todd Herzog
- Chana Rothman
- Josh Nelson
- Six13
- Ross M. Levy
- Cantor Billy Tiep
- Mikey Pauker
- Beth Schafer
- Noam Katz
- Bryan Zive and Kol Echad
- Cantor Michael Smolash and Ari Posner
- Sababa
- Sam Glaser
- Eric Komar
- Felicia Lilien

**Ruach 5767**  Featuring 19 tunes from:
- Sheldon Low
- Dan Nichols
- Stacy Beyer
- Rick Recht
- Josh Nelson
- Debbie Friedman
- Noam Katz
- Six13
- Mah Tovu
- Peri Smilow & The Freedom Music Project
- Mark Aaron James
- Beth Schafer
- Ross M. Levy
- Steve Dropkin
- Sue Horowitz
- The Israeli Mechina's *Zimrat Yah*
- Eric Komar

**Ruach 5765: Israel**  Featuring 13 tunes from:
- Noam Katz
- HaDag Nachash
- Dan Nichols
- Aviv Gefen
- Stacy Beyer
- Rick Recht
- Yom Hadash
- The Fools of Prophecy
- Beth Schafer
- Steve Dropkin
- Neal Katz
- Sheva
- Teapacks

**Ruach 5763/61**  Featuring 27 tunes from:
- Dan Nichols & Eighteen
- Steve Dropkin
- Peri Smilow
- Mah Tovu
- Rick Recht
- Danny Maseng
- Cantor Wally
- Jeff Klepper
- Julie Silver
- Craig Taubman
- Beth Schafer
- Debbie Friedman
- Noam Katz
- Yom Hadash